Published by The Museum of Science and History, Little Rock, Arkansas

To Susan

The structure now housing the Museum of Science and History in MacArthur Park in Little Rock was built between 1838-1840 and is the only structure remaining of the 27-building Little Rock Arsenal. The Arsenal was closed in 1890, but it was not until 1942 that the building was made into a museum.

Overleaf: "Cuttin' rice" on the Grand Prairie near Stuttgart, farmers run a harvest marathon that lasts till sunset and beyond.

Page 1: Twelve-year-old Tabitha Spikes practices violin at Bayou Meto School near Jacksonville. She is in her second year of an Arkansas Symphony program designed to introduce orchestral string instruments to students in the public schools.

Second Edition, October, 1984.
Library of Congress Catalog Card Number: 80-81993. ISBN: 0-9604642-0-4 Regular Edition; ISBN: 0-9604642-1-2 Limited Gift Edition.

FOREWORD

First Edition 1980

"In 1836 Governor Conway made a plea to the War Department for an arsenal in Arkansas. After a takeover by state authorities, occupation by Confederate forces, a surrender to advancing Federal forces in 1863, and the birth of General Douglas MacArthur, the arsenal was closed."

These words serve as a legend to a photomural in the foyer of The Museum of Science and History, which now occupies the Tower Building, the only surviving structure of the Little Rock Arsenal, which operated from 1836 to 1890.

In 1942 permission was given to move The Museum of Natural History and Antiquities from City Hall to the Tower Building. This was the beginning of an effort to provide scientific, historic, and educational resources and to stimulate an awareness of the environmental and cultural heritage of Arkansas.

The sun has set on the building as an arsenal, as a part of a city park, as the birthplace of a famous general, and as a museum without at theme. A period for decision, a time for bold steps in serving the public in new and innovative ways arose in the 1970s. Decisions have been made and the steps are being taken, through the interest and devotion of citizens serving on the Board of Trustees, through the role of The Museum in statewide educational programs, and through a concerned public.

Renovation of interior spaces of the building was begun in the mid-1970s. This was accompanied by an air of development, a sense of purpose, and new plans based on the decision to have a museum dedicated to the theme "Arkansas, Its Land and People." It is from this theme that all new programming at The Museum will emerge.

Recent and exhaustive research on this theme has resulted in more than 280 "stories" to be told by The permanent and temporary exhibits, multi-media programs, publications, classroom presentations, public lectures, and television programming.

The Museum is now dedicated to a melding of the natural sciences and the cultural history of Arkansas. Therefore, all of the public offerings of The Museum emphasizing the relationship between people and the land and the quality of life in Arkansas.

The Museum is proud to make this book available to the public. First, because *Arkansas, Its Land and People* is the product of Matt Bradley, an Arkansan who has published in notable national and international works. And second, because the title refers to the future of The Museum.

Thus, The Museum enters the decade of the 1980s with a twenty-five year plan to serve "Arkansas, Its Land and People." This book is the first step in that plan.

Richard J. Baldauf, Ph.D.
Executive Director, 1978-1983
The Museum of Science and History

Second Edition 1984

The Arkansas Museum of Science and History is pleased to present a second edition of ARKANSAS, ITS LAND AND PEOPLE. This photographic collection captures the essence of Arkansas as a land of natural beauty, plentiful resources, and contrasting ways of life—a refuge for vacationing and retiring Americans.

ARKANSAS, ITS LAND AND PEOPLE focuses upon the close relationship between a people and their land, and is symbolic of The Museum's approach to science and history. The Museum's message is one of concern for the environment and for the public's need to understand the forces which shaped the past and will shape the future. A spectacular view of Arkansas, with special effects of thunderstorms drenching the land with precious water, is presented in The Museum's popular mini-theater. Book and film both illustrate the importance of preserving the delicate balance between Arkansas as "A Natural" and as a "Land of Opportunity".

The struggle between preservation and conservation and economic growth and development can be resolved if we use our ingenuity. As the last decade of the 20th Century approaches, the goal of the Arkansas Museum of Science and History is to help produce a public well informed of scientific and historical developments who will be able to participate in making crucial decisions concerning the future.

While continuing in the tradition of museums as educational institutions which collect and preserve objects of significance, the Board of Trustees is committed to creative new developments. Its mission is to produce a first rate museum for Arkansas, one with interactive displays which will elicit the joy of learning and enhance the quality of life this book extols.

Alison B. Sanchez, Ph.D.
Executive Director
The Arkansas Museum of Science and History

CONTENTS

No work and all play – that is the law laid down by schoolmarm Delanna Crymes (right) at the Little School House, part of the Ozark Folk Center near Mountain View. Visiting youngsters spin tops, dance stick puppets, and challenge the charming headmistress to the old-fashioned game of foxes and geese, played with acorns and corn kernels.

THE LAND

Sixty-five feet from floor to ceiling, the Giant Column dwarfs a tour group walking the Dripstone Trail in Blanchard Springs Caverns. The Caverns are probably the largest of hundreds of caves – known and unknown – that lie deep under the Arkansas Ozarks.

Ozark travelers face a dilemma: how to stay on twisting, dipping roads while enjoying scenery both natural and man-made. On Highway 23 – commonly known as "the Pig Trail" – cyclists wind along a leafy tunnel north of Cass, while on Highway 71 a painted barn ministers to a congregation of speeding motorists near Fayetteville.

Nestled in the mountainous folds of Newton County is the valley of Boxley – an emerald carpet given a New England touch by the old schoolhouse

and church. With the coming of high water in the
spring, canoeists launch from Boxley into an Eden-like
setting, the Buffalo National River (following pages).

A thirty-foot fall of maidenhair ferns graces the bank of the Buffalo near Mount Hersey.

In an early morning fog, gravel bar campers warm themselves by a breakfast fire. ▶

It is hard to imagine the upper Buffalo River without Granny Henderson. For so many years she and her cabin and her animals were part of the landscape near Hemmed-in Hollow.

Granny's life mirrored the resoluteness of earlier pioneers. Alone, without the amenities of running water or electricity, she devoted much of her time to her animals. Every day she carried buckets of water from the river for her cattle. Some folks said she had the best hogs in Newton County.

Old barns (following pages), log cabins, and fieldstone chimneys are fast disappearing, but among those who knew and loved Granny Henderson, her spirit remains.

At Hemmed-in Hollow the highest waterfall between the Appalachians and the Rockies plummets two hundred feet from the rim of a box canyon. Seen from below on a sunny day, the water is an endless stream of diamonds falling in slow motion, swaying and weaving in the wind.

Lowering themselves on a rope next to the falls, rappelers descend like spiders on a single thread, also subject to the vagaries of the wind.

Noon is a good time to arrive at the general store at Gilbert, just a short walk from the Buffalo's left bank. In the store's cool interior, the sandwiches taste awfully good, especially after a morning of paddling in the sun. Then the day's mail arrives at the post office, and the locals show up to check their boxes and ''sit for a spell,'' catching up on the news.

Seen from the air, the rice fields of the Grand Prairie and the Delta of eastern Arkansas are a delight to the eye, as newly-raised levees curve and swirl on a richly textured background.

In the fall when weather conditions and moisture content are right, harvest crews run their combines far into the night (following pages).

Rice waits under tarpaulins in the dusk at the grain dryer in Altheimer. "Largest number of trucks we've ever had in the yard," says manager Terry Stephens. "It's taking pretty near two full days to unload, now." Once the rice is weighed and off-loaded, it is transported by bucket elevator to men like Tommy Watkins (right), "hot-house man" at a mill in Stuttgart.

Watkins works on the second floor of the dryer, a world of high temperatures and swirling dust.

Mechanized farming leaves enough grain in the fields to feed thousands of waterfowl funneling down the Mississippi Flyway each fall, thus providing a secondary harvest for Arkansas hunters (following pages).

Raymond Schroeder and Junior Cook both know catfish, but when it comes to eating the whiskered creature, they are poles apart. Schroeder is a former Catfish-Farmer-of-the-Year whose ponds (above) are located near Carlisle. Cook is a life-long commercial fisherman who plies the Arkansas River (left).

"River fish taste the best," grunts Cook.

"Any day of the week, pond-raised are better," Schroeder replies.

And so the great Catfish Controversy rages. But it is a battle that any catfish-eater can take pleasure in, especially when the fare (from either river or pond) is rolled in light batter, cooked in grease that's hot enough to light a match, and served with generous portions of purple onions, hushpuppies and cole slaw.

47

50

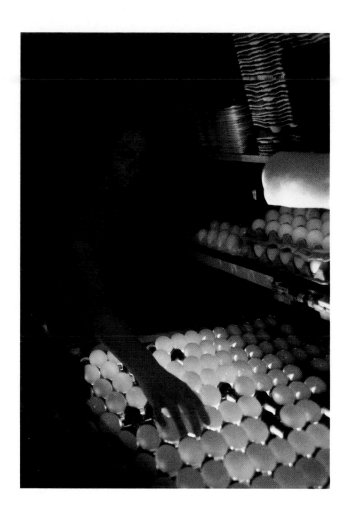

The Atkins Pickle Company has more than 400 holding tanks, each with a capacity of 350 to 1000 bushels. "More often than not, I end up in the tanks pushing pickles!" laughs dock foreman Tim Pugh.

At Tyson Foods' egg plant in Springdale, a candler removes the checks (cracked eggs), dirts (dirty eggs) and B-grades before the best are packed for table use.

Jack Brashears checks the feeders in his 16,000-bird chicken house. ▶

On an oil rig between El Dorado and Magnolia, roughnecks "go back in the hole" after changing a bit.

Sailboat spinnakers color the horizon during a downwind leg at Lake Maumelle. ▶

The sport of fishing takes many forms, from a lone fisherman in a flatbottom boat to dozens competing in a professional bass-fishing tournament. Here at Lake Ouachita, the early morning line-up is an armada of sleek high-horsepower craft with blinking displays of electronics. Some participants wear crash helmets. Even if one doesn't land many fish, he can at least make an impressive start.

THE PEOPLE

Meg and Amanda Williams, twins and newcomers to Eureka Springs, await the coming of Halloween amid autumn color in the restored Victorian town.

matched state-wide whenever the Razorbacks take the
field or court.

*Everybody hopes to be a winner at Hot Springs'
Oaklawn Jockey Club. In the stands, Alyne Herring of
Albuquerque sports a lucky ring on every finger, while*
*in the stables, high-strung thoroughbred Gas-a-Gas
seeks reassurance from Herman, his stablemate and
traveling companion.*

Ah, those long lazy days of childhood summer! How fervently they are longed for in the spring. How slowly they sometimes pass ...

In Arkansas City, summertime buddies gather on the corner by the Red Star Grocery to decide what to do next: go fishing at Kate Adams Lake, swim at the Third Pothole, or go to the library (" ... 'cause that's where all the girls are").

Twelve-year-old Chris Ginn's best girl, Fanny, usually rides on his shoulders as he pedals around Pine Bluff.

Small-town festivals in Arkansas have a genuine quality without pretense of grandeur and with little commercialism.

During Warren's Pink Tomato Festival each June, the Bradley County Courthouse square swarms with activity following the parade: tomato bobbing, wrist wrestling, a tomato-eating contest, and a talent competition staged on a flatbed trailer. Everyone is invited to attend the all-tomato luncheon at the Methodist Church. And later in the day, some of the most bewitching beauties in the world vie for the title of Little Miss Pink Tomato. ▶

Handmade ... homegrown. Country folks know how to make do. Ingenuity is a way of life, and money is seldom exchanged for goods and services.

Gene Waters and his family live in a small farmhouse on 58 acres near Cabot. His business card reads "Waters Enterprises," a variety of activities that include truck driving, cow farming, house renting and scrap-metal gathering. "A little bit of this and a little bit of that," he says. Every fall, Waters brings his sorghum cane to the mill off Highway 5 near El Paso (left) for the sweet juice to be extracted and boiled into molasses. For his help, the mill's owner retains a portion of the syrup.

Orphea Duty (above) is a matriarch of hospitality at Boxley. When 78 years of age she still covered five counties in northern Arkansas selling Tupperware. Now she devotes most of her energy to the Walnut Grove Baptist Church, her iris garden, and baking banana nut bread, much of which she feeds to the birds. "They like raisin pie pretty well, too," she says.

"I always felt locked-up in the city," Sheri Phillips-Chisholm says. "Gerry and I came to Mountain View with twenty-seven hundred dollars. We wanted to build our own home and be close to birds and animals."

Since arriving in Arkansas, the two Tennessee natives have done just that. Their two-story home, built of stone and situated in a deep wooded valley near Mountain View, is nearly finished. And they are close to the birds and animals . . . both real and wooden, for along the way they have become successful woodcarvers.

Intricately carved birds perch along their workshop shelves. A raccoon fashioned from buckeye-wood peers up from washing a fish. A frightened baby cottontail huddles in a corner – so real it must be touched to believe it is wood. Outside the workshop window, real songbirds flutter around the feeders.

About eight in the morning, after feeding the ducks and the chickens, the couple begin to carve. After a lunch break they continue carving till past five – long past, if they are preparing for a show. For relaxation they read, or play the dulcimer with friends.

"When we first came to Arkansas, we were hoping to be welcomed," Sheri says. "And we were. These have been the happiest years of my life."

"I wasn't cut out to be a musician, but I'm handy with tools," admits Florian Thurston, a 74-year-old fiddle maker from Leslie. Two of his most recent instruments decorate the wall of a tack shed next to his workshop. "I'm going to raise my price pretty soon," he says. "I may not sell too many fiddles, but I'll get to look at them longer that way."

The custom-made knives of Jimmy Lile of Russellville have earned him the title of The Arkansas Knifesmith.

With chaw in cheek and hands on his steering "sticks," Danny Askue guides the harbor tug John L. Murphy toward a waiting tow of barges on the Mississippi River near Osceola. His son Joey watches. ▶

By day, downtown Little Rock radiates small-town casualness and warmth. Office workers munch sandwiches on the mall at noon; friends meet and chat on sidewalks and in elevators. But in the evening as the lights blink on, the town takes on a big-city feeling. The buildings seem taller and more imposing.

This big-city spell is broken only at Christmas, when the Capitol is decked in holiday color. ▶

Country comes to the city at the Little Rock farmer's market, with its delightful fragrance of fresh produce. Vendors give careful attention to fair

*measure and – unlike the supermarket – many allow
a taste test.*

Charles and Becky Witsell remove outer layers of finish from a bannister in the 1889-vintage Frederick Hanger House. They have spent over eight years restoring the Quapaw Quarter home, rejuvenating such details as ivory-and-gilt parlor woodwork, ceiling decorations, gaslights and stained glass.

A water-skier carves a golden wake across the Little Maumelle inlet area of the Arkansas River in northwest Little Rock. ▶

Holly Patrick has one of the most difficult parts imaginable for an eight-year-old actress. Playing a green toy rabbit in Geppetto's toy shop, she must

remain motionless until she is suddenly brought to
life. The play is Pinocchio, a Children's Theater
production at the Arkansas Arts Center.

The midway at the fair! The young watch wide-eyed. Everybody's senses come alive. The air seems electrically charged by the swirling colored lights. Nowhere else are colors more vibrant, the screams of thrill-riders more piercing. Nowhere else does cotton candy taste so good.

"We've known each other ever since the Ark landed," Hale Garner laughs as he trims a customer's hair. Garner's barber shop in Calico Rock hasn't

changed much over the years. The beveled-glass
mirror reflects the same chair and equipment it did
when he opened the shop 41 years ago.

"I suppose farming has always been in my blood. One of my grandfathers was a sawmiller. The other was a sharecropper who farmed cotton with mules until he was 70. I used to help him in the summer."

After earning a masters degree in history and teaching for two years at Vanderbilt, Billy Higgins purchased 120 acres in a remote side-valley of the Little Mulberry River. He and his wife Peggy have 35 acres in hay and field corn, raise cattle and hogs, keep bees, and help operate a small sawmill.

"We try to run a family farm," says Higgins. "Everyone has a job to do around here, even the cats. They keep the corncrib free of mice."

The rocky Ozarks have always been hills of hard times, reflected here in the faces of 68-year-old Orvil "Strawberry" Henson and two of his 16 children, who live near Winslow.

Twenty-two-year-old Bert Pouncey takes a break from disking a field near Greasy Corner, east of Forrest City – soil that has been farmed by his family for four generations. "I've got one and a half, maybe two weeks at most before my beans burn plumb up," he moans. "I'm not even putting on herbicide this year. If my crop burns up, that would be just that much more money I'd have to come up with."

Moving across his field again, Pouncey and his tractor disappear in a cloud of dust.

At the end of a long day, agricultural pilot Pete Hartman of Wilson refuels with 60 gallons of 80/87 octane. ▶

As the bidding slows for an ancient pickup truck at a farm equipment sale near DeWitt, auctioneer Tom Blackmon halts his singsong chant for a moment:

"Now come on fellas, you know the prettiest girls
don't always dance the best!" The truck sells.

With only his thoughts and a swarm of mosquitoes for company, Teddy Widen lantern-fishes on Lake Conway. "Every chance I get, I'm out on that lake," he says. "You can always find a bass or two hanging around those log jams."

Teddy's father Ted Widen retired in Arkansas after 26 years in the Air Force, and he and his family now run Adams Lake Boat Dock on Lake Conway . . . with the help of a cat that never strays far from the minnow tank.

PHOTOGRAPHER'S NOTES

In the course of my photography, the pictures that I remember best seem to fall into two categories — those that I have to work at to achieve, and those that I steal. Well, I don't mean steal literally, but rather in the sense of making the most of a chance or an opportunity.

For example, late one steamy August afternoon I was driving back to Little Rock from a lengthy assignment in the Ozarks. Arm out the window, shirt sticking to my back, I was thinking about getting home and finding something cold to drink. Then, when crossing the Arkansas River on the Interstate 430 bridge, I happened to glance over the railing to the right. The sinking sun had transformed the water below into a river of molten gold. And on its surface skimmed a water-skier, his wake a graceful curve of sparkling highlights. Without hesitation I stopped.

At times like these, when a picture requires immediate attention if it's to be captured, my actions result not so much from conscious thought as from reflexes: load film, change lens, set shutter and aperture, and get into position. The composition in the camera viewfinder is more felt than seen; it either feels right or it doesn't.

The river scene felt right, and was so easily recorded I felt a little guilty. It was a beautiful moment, just there for the taking, the dust jacket photograph of this book ... and I stole it.

But not all photographs come so easily. The picture of Blanchard Springs Caverns on page 9 took three full days of work: previsualization, composition, tedious adjustments of the cave's lighting with other lights added where needed, and test exposures.

The final exposures were closely coordinated with prearranged signals transmitted by walkie-talkies. Two Blanchard Springs maintenance technicians served as photographic assistants; one held a strobe and the other manipulated the computerized spotlight that illuminated the Giant Column. The guide and his tour group were flashed with strobes when they reached the designated position, and the spotlight was turned on for precisely eight seconds. When the light was switched off, the people moved quickly down the steps and behind the Giant Column for the duration of the time exposure, which lasted a full three minutes. My work seemed closer to a time/motion management exercise than simply tripping a shutter!

As I have traveled around Arkansas and become familiar with the state's land and people, I have learned something else — the memorable pictures come more readily in Arkansas than in other places I have visited. The reason lies somewhere beyond the landscapes, the spectacular caves and pretty sunsets. It has more to do with the home-cooked meals I've been offered, the many times that strangers have gone out of their way to help me. Perhaps it stems, too, from my own family roots deep in the soil of the southeast Arkansas delta.

Whatever the reason, I firmly believe there is no better place to live and work than Arkansas. But then I suppose it's only natural to feel that the grass of home is a little greener ... and the pictures just a little easier to steal.

Matt Bradley

Little Rock
July, 1980

Nature's dripping palette, a sandstone bluff at Pruitt on the Buffalo National River, displays subtle coloration.

ACKNOWLEDGMENTS

Special thanks are due to Dick Baldauf, former director of the Museum of Science and History, and Sam Bracy of Peerless Engravers, whose interest and support are in large part responsible for this book.

Additional credit should be given to the following organizations whose interest helped make this second edition of *Arkansas, Its Land and People* a reality:

Systematics, Inc.
First Arkansas Bankstock Corporation
Orbit Valve Company
Worthen Bank and Trust Company
Arkansas Electric Cooperatives
Central Flying Service
Arkansas Modification Center Inc.
Arkansas Louisiana Gas Company
Arkansas Power & Light Company
Little Rock Convention & Visitors Bureau
University of Arkansas Medical Sciences

Southwestern Bell Telephone Company
Arkansas Bankers Association
Arthur Young and Company
Department of Parks and Tourism
Pickens-Bond Construction Company
University of Arkansas at Pine Bluff
Alcoa-Aluminum Company of America
Rebsamen Insurance
Rector-Phillips-Morse
First National Bank of Stuttgart
Farmers and Merchants Bank of Stuttgart

Color Separations: Peerless Engraving Company
Printing: International Graphics Industries
Typesetting: Diversitype-Diversified Graphics

Editing: Kenneth L. Smith (Fayetteville), Ralph Patrick
Design: Bruce Wesson
Production Art: Jonathan Hay Smith